Finley Miles Darby Meets the Bisons at Yellowstone

Michael S. Joyner, MD

Hand Surgeon, Inventor & Author

Dr. Michael Joyner, a Los Angeles native, graduated from Georgetown University School of Medicine in Washington, DC as a United States Army Health Scholarship Recipient. He completed his general surgery internship at Walter Reed Army Medical Center where he served active duty as a captain in the United States Army. His undergraduate degree is from Howard University. Dr. Joyner is also the inventor of Touchless Flatware and Touchless Chopsticks. He is the founder of Forever My Daddy Grand Foundation. And he operates thriving Hand Surgery practices in Florida and Nebraska. The FMD Book series is dedicated to parents who believe in co-parenting.

Finley Miles Darby Meets the Bisons at Yellowstone

Copyright 2023 by Forever My Daddy, LLC

Finley Miles Darby Meets the Bisons at Yellowstone

All rights reserved. No part of this publication may be reproduced, distributed, or transmitted in any form or by any means, including photocopying, recording, or other electronic or mechanical methods, without the prior written permission of the publisher, except in the case of brief quotations embodied in critical reviews and certain other noncommercial uses permitted by copyright law. For permission requests, email to the publisher, addressed "Attention: Permissions Coordinator," to Foevermydaddy@gmail.com.

ISBN: 979-8-9867716-7-0

Forever My Daddy LLC

Printed in the United States of America

First Printing, 2023

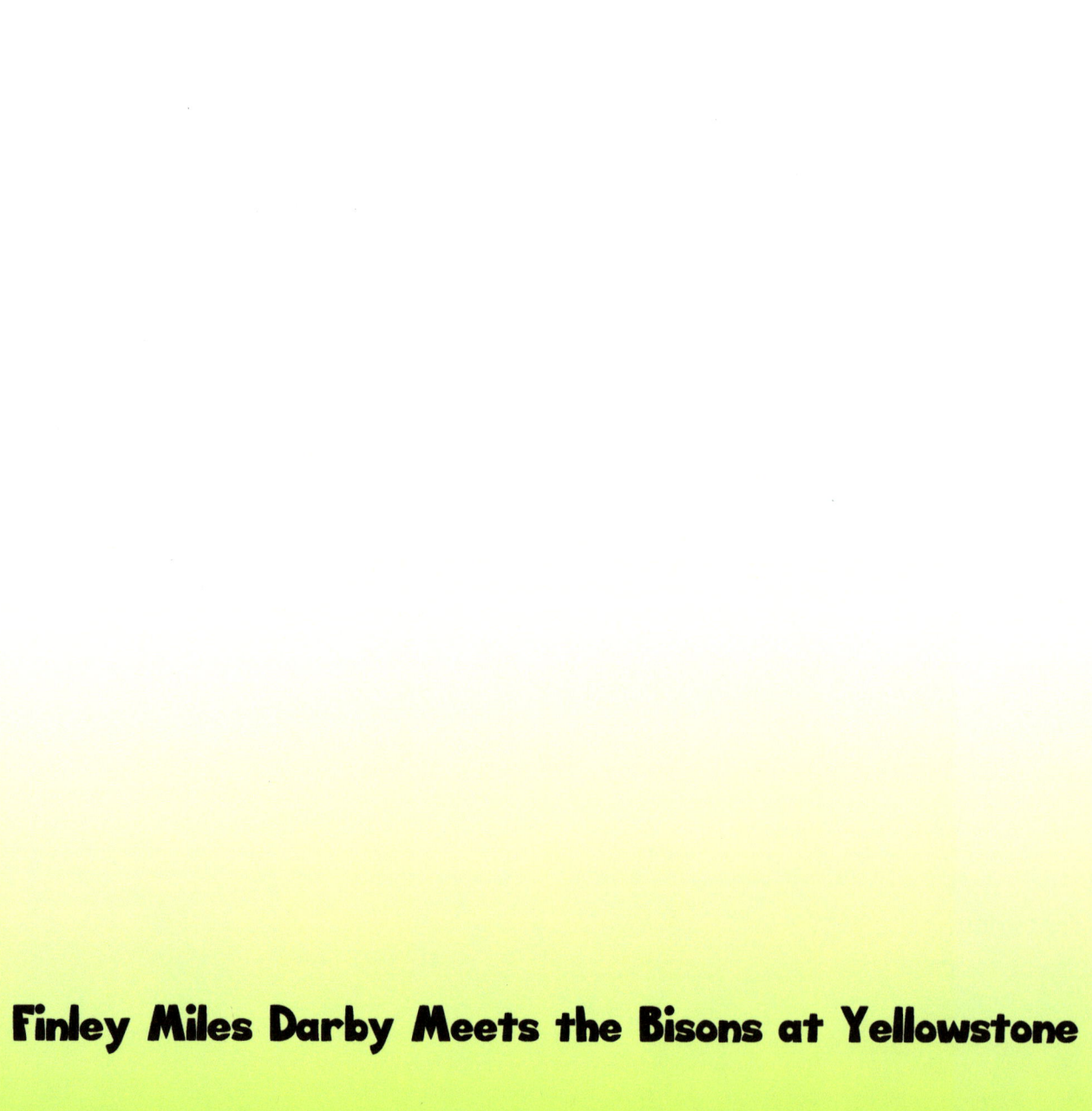

Finley Miles Darby Meets the Bisons at Yellowstone

**Meet
Finley Miles Darby**

Finley loves getting to know his Father. His parents are in a co-parenting relationship. He did not spend much time with his Father before he decided that he wanted to get to know him.

In the FMD Book Series, Finley shares his experiences with his best friends, his dogs Zen and Buddha. After each visit, Finley highlights the stories and memories he makes with his Father.

"Yay! Another fun weekend calls for another great adventure, and I'm sure this one has taught him a lot!"
said Zen the Newfoundland as he saw Finley approaching the house after another weekend with his father.

"Oh, I'm so excited!" exclaimed Buddha the Frenchy.

Finley arrived as they were talking.
"Hey, my two best friends! I really missed you!"
"We missed you as well!"
"Did you have a good
weekend with your father?"
Zen, the Newfoundland, inquired.

"Oh, yes! This weekend was without a doubt the best!"

"Oh, please tell us!" Please tell us!"
Buddha the Frenchy begged.

"All right, guys, all right!
Relax and pay attention to everything I've learned!"
said Finley, as they sat down to talk.

"I went to Yellowstone National Park this weekend."
"Have you heard of it?"

"Oh, yes!"
exclaimed Buddha the Frenchy.

"I believe I've heard of it. It's a large park."
"Yes, Frenchy, it is. Furthermore, it is the world's first national park."
"Wow! Finley, that must have been an incredible journey!

Zen the Newfoundland states,
"Please tell us about the park!"

"There were many unique hydrothermal and geologic features in the park.
I got to see wildlife, explore geothermal areas with half of the world's active geysers, and see geologic wonders like the Yellowstone River's Grand Canyon.
It was an absolutely breathtaking journey!"

"Oh, how I wish I could have been there!" exclaimed Buddha the Frenchy.

"You must have learned a lot by closely watching them."

"Indeed, Buddha!"
The bison, on the other hand,
was the most interesting animal I saw.
"Do you have any idea what a bison is?"

"Hmm, never heard of it!"
Buddha the Frenchy exclaimed.

"Do you, Zen?"
Zen the Newfoundland exclaimed,

"Never in my life!"

"Well, bisons are North America's largest
land-dwelling mammal.
Males are larger than females,
and both have dark chocolate-brown hair on
their forelegs, head, and shoulders,
but short, dense hair on their flanks
and hindquarters."

"Wow, that sounds like an interesting animal!"
exclaimed Buddha the Frenchy.

"They are very cool, Frenchy!"
However, there is more.
Bisons are fast swimmers and can run at speeds of up to 35 miles per hour.
They can jump over 5 foot high objects and have excellent hearing, vision, and smell."

"But how does a bison spend his day?"
Zen the Newfoundland inquired.

"Very good question, Zen!"
Finley exclaimed.

"Bisons are mostly active during the day and at dusk, but they can be active all night."
They are social animals that frequently form herds that appear to be led by older females. In the winter, groups of 20 bison are common, but in the summer, groups of 200 bison are common. Throughout the year, Yellowstone bison feed primarily on grasses, sedges, and other grass-like plants (more than 90% of their diet) in open grassland and meadow communities."

"They're awesome!"
exclaimed Buddha the Frenchy.

"Did you also know something interesting about bison?"
Finley inquired.

"No, but please tell us!" Finley, tell us!"
Zen the Newfoundland asked.

"The bison is Howard University's mascot."

"Wow, but why is that?"
Zen the Newfoundland inquired.

"Well, the Howard Bison, named after one of America's first national mammals, represent pride, history, intelligence, resilience and power,"
Finley explained.

"I see!"
Zen, the Newfoundland, responded.

"Well, this has to be one of the most incredible things you've taught us. Right, Buddha?"

"We as always are always so excited
about the time that you spend
with your father.
We know that you and your father
are building history.
We are so glad that you reached out to him
and that you are open to
developing a relationship with him,"
says Zen.

"Of course, we already can't wait
until you spend more time with him.
We love to hear your stories!"
exclaimed Buddha

...END...

Do you like to color these illustrations?
Checkout the coloring book!

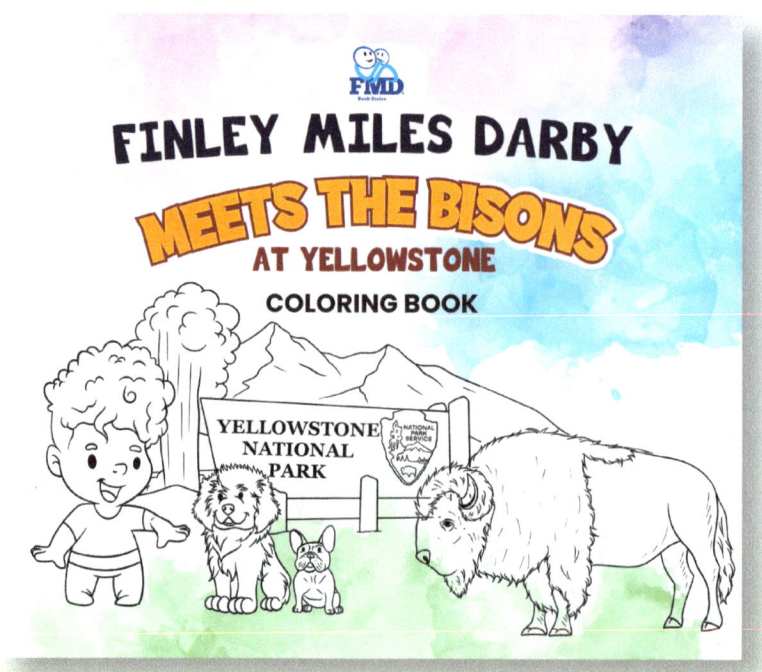

Order now on Amazon : https://a.co/d/cmpfadY

Did you miss others of FMD series?

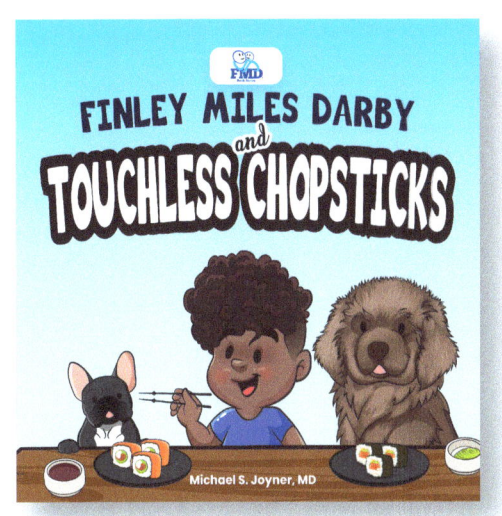

Order now on Amazon :
https://a.co/d/5TvBYE7

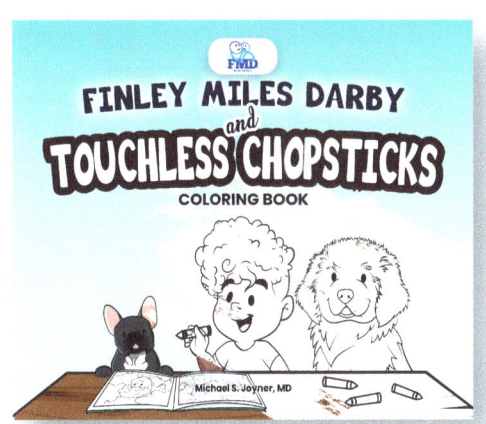

Order now on Amazon :
https://a.co/d/bNBMuHu

www.ingramcontent.com/pod-product-compliance
Lightning Source LLC
Chambersburg PA
CBHW040726060526
44119CB00084B/340